Stupid Leader

Paulette Durand

Paulette Durand

Paulette Durand

Copyright Page

Legal and legal data
Copyright holder: © 2024, Roberto Albira
Year: 2024
Author: © Paulette Durand

No part of this book may be reproduced, stored in a retrieval system, or transmitted in any form or by any means, electronic, mechanical, photocopying, recording, or otherwise, without the prior written permission of the author or publisher. . . Brief quotations in critical reviews and certain other non-commercial uses are permitted as permitted by copyright law.

Index

Paulette Durand

What is a Stupid Leader?

A stupid leader is a figure that, unfortunately, many of us have encountered throughout our professional lives. He is that person in a position of authority who seems to make all the wrong decisions, no matter how clear and obvious the correct alternatives are. But what really defines a stupid leader? Let's break it down.

First, a stupid leader is someone who makes impulsive decisions without considering the long-term consequences. This type of leader acts without thinking, moved by whims or momentary emotions. He imagines a captain of a ship who, in the middle of a storm, decides to change course because he feels that the wind has calmed down a little, without consulting any map or taking into account weather forecasts. This is how a stupid leader acts in the corporate world: without data, without analysis and, above all, without thinking about the future.

Another hallmark of a stupid leader is lack of vision. This leader cannot see beyond the immediate and does not have a clear strategic plan. He is like a chess player who only thinks about his next move, without foreseeing how it will affect the entire game. In a company, this translates into poorly managed projects, wasted resources and, ultimately, guaranteed failure.

Communication is another Achilles heel of a stupid leader. This type of leader does not know how to communicate effectively. His instructions are confusing, his expectations are unclear, and when problems arise, the blame always falls on others. There is no place for transparency or open dialogue. A stupid leader simply doesn't listen, and when he does, he doesn't understand.

A stupid leader is also characterized by an excessive ego. He believes himself to be infallible and superior to everyone else. This type of leader does not accept criticism or advice, and any suggestion that contradicts his opinion is seen as a threat. Instead of fostering an environment of collaboration and learning, he imposes his will in an authoritarian manner, dampening the team's creativity and motivation.

Lack of empathy is another clear sign of a stupid leader. He does not understand or care about the needs and feelings of his employees. For him, workers are not people with aspirations and problems of their own, but mere cogs in the company's machinery. This emotional disconnection creates a toxic work environment, where demotivation and resentment flourish.

Furthermore, a stupid leader rarely learns from his mistakes. Instead of reflecting on his failures and seeking to improve, he remains in constant denial, repeating the same mistakes over and over again. This lack of self-criticism perpetuates a cycle of mediocrity and failure, both for him and for the organization he leads.

Finally, a stupid leader has no integrity. He is dishonest, manipulates the truth to his convenience and does not keep his promises. This lack of ethics erodes the trust of its employees, partners and clients, irreparably damaging the company's reputation.

In short, a stupid leader is a mixture of impulsivity, lack of vision, poor communication, excessive ego, lack of empathy, inability to learn and lack of integrity. These defects not only affect him as an individual, but also drag his team and his organization to failure. Recognizing these characteristics is the first step in avoiding becoming a stupid leader and in fostering more conscious and effective leadership.

Impulsive Decisions and Without Data

One of the most common and destructive mistakes a stupid leader can make is making impulsive decisions without being based on data. Imagine being in an airplane and realizing that the pilot decides to turn sharply without consulting the instruments, simply because he feels it is the right thing to do. It's a scary idea, right? Well, this is how many leaders lead their organizations to disaster, trusting their instincts instead of the information available.

Impulsive decisions are usually emotional reactions to pressure situations. When a leader does not take the time to analyze the data and reflect on the possible consequences, he is gambling with the future of the company. For example, a leader may decide to launch a new product on the market without conducting prior studies or pilot testing, simply because he believes it is a good idea. However, this lack of preparation can lead to dismal failure, with significant economic losses and irreparable damage to the company's reputation.

Take the case of a technology company that decided to launch a new device without extensive testing. The leader, excited by the novelty and pressured by the competition, gave the green light without considering the warnings of his development team. The result was a bug-ridden product that not only disappointed customers, but also generated huge costs in returns and repairs. All of this could have been avoided with a little patience and data analysis.

Impulsive decisions can also arise from overconfidence. Some leaders believe that their intuition is infallible and that they can make complex decisions in a matter of seconds. This attitude is not only arrogant, but also dangerous. A smart leader knows that intuition can be useful, but that it must always be backed by hard data. Without data, a decision becomes a simple bet, and in the business world, betting is a very risky game.

Additionally, when a leader makes impulsive decisions, he or she sends a negative message to his or her team. Employees begin to doubt the leader's ability to handle critical situations and lose confidence in their decisions. This can lead to a climate of uncertainty and demotivation, where the team feels insecure about the direction of the company. A leader who acts without data undermines group morale and cohesion, creating a toxic work environment.

A classic example of impulsive, data-deprived decisions can be seen in corporate mergers and acquisitions. Sometimes a leader gets carried away by the desire for rapid expansion and buys another company without doing due diligence. Without a detailed evaluation of the assets, liabilities, and corporate culture of the target company, the merger can turn out to be disastrous. Cultural conflicts, hidden financial problems, and unmet expectations can turn a seemingly brilliant decision into a huge failure.

So how can a leader avoid falling into the trap of impulsive decisions? The answer is simple: take the time to collect and analyze relevant data. Before making an important decision, a leader must seek all available information, consult with experts, and consider all possible consequences. It's not about slowing down the decision-making process to the point of paralysis, but rather ensuring that each decision is well-informed.

Planning and foresight are key. A leader must have a clear, long-term vision, and every decision must align with this vision. It is essential to establish decision-making processes and protocols that include data collection, risk analysis, and evaluation of alternatives. These processes not only help make better decisions, but also foster a culture of responsibility and care in the organization.

In conclusion, impulsive and dataless decisions are one of the main characteristics of a stupid leader. These decisions can have devastating consequences for the company and the team. The key to avoiding this mistake is to take a data-driven approach, carefully think through each decision, and always maintain a long-term view. Responsible and effective leadership is based on information and analysis, not intuition and impulsivity.

Lack of Vision and Strategic Planning

One of the most critical mistakes a stupid leader can make is lacking vision and strategic planning. Without a clear direction and a plan to get there, any organization is destined to fail. A leader without vision is like a ship captain who sails aimlessly in the middle of the ocean, letting himself be carried away by the currents and winds without knowing where he is going. This is not only dangerous, but also irresponsible.

The vision is the starting point of any effective strategy. It is the clear and motivating image of what the organization wants to achieve in the future. A leader with vision knows where he wants to take his team and has a clear idea of how to get there. However, a stupid leader lacks this vision. He does not have a clear idea of the future and, therefore, he cannot inspire or guide his team towards a common goal.

Lack of vision manifests itself in making short-term decisions without considering the long-term implications. This type of leader focuses on solving immediate problems without thinking about how their decisions will affect the future of the organization. For example, he may cut spending on research and development to increase short-term profits, without realizing that this compromises long-term innovation and competitiveness.

In addition to vision, strategic planning is essential for success. Strategic planning involves defining clear objectives, identifying necessary resources and establishing an action plan to achieve those objectives. A stupid leader doesn't take the time to plan strategically. Instead, he acts reactively, responding to crises as they arise without a long-term plan.

Imagine a company that wants to expand into a new market without conducting a thorough analysis of that market. Without proper planning, the company may face problems such as lack of demand, fierce competition, and cultural differences that it had not anticipated. This can result in significant resource loss and failure of expansion. Proper strategic planning would have identified these risks and prepared the company to deal with them effectively.

The lack of vision and strategic planning is also reflected in the inability to anticipate and adapt to market changes. A stupid leader is not attentive to trends and changes in his industry. This means that the organization may fall behind while its competitors advance. For example, many companies that did not see the potential of e-commerce early on were left behind while others quickly adopted the technology and dominated the market.

Another crucial aspect of strategic planning is resource management. A leader without strategic planning does not know how to allocate resources efficiently. This can lead to an ineffective allocation of resources, where some areas of the business are overstretched while others lack what they need to operate. A stupid leader can invest large amounts of money in projects that have no future while neglecting crucial areas such as talent development and innovation.

Lack of vision and strategic planning also has a negative impact on team morale. Employees want to know where the company is going and how their efforts contribute to that goal. Without a clear vision and strategic plan, employees can feel lost and demotivated. Not knowing what the end goal is makes daily work seem meaningless and reduces team cohesion and commitment.

To avoid this mistake, a leader must develop a clear vision and communicate it to the entire team. This vision must be inspiring and achievable, and must align with the organization's values and objectives. In addition, the leader must dedicate time to strategic planning, establishing long-term objectives and defining a detailed action plan to achieve them. This includes conducting an in-depth analysis of the market, identifying opportunities and threats, and allocating resources efficiently.

In conclusion, the lack of vision and strategic planning is a serious mistake that can lead to the failure of any organization. A stupid leader who does not have a clear direction and does not plan for the long term is condemning his team to navigate aimlessly in a sea of uncertainty. To be an effective leader, it is essential to have an inspiring vision and a solid strategic plan that guides the organization to long-term success.

Paulette Durand

Negligence in Change Management

One of the biggest mistakes a stupid leader can make is being negligent in managing change. In the business world, change is inevitable. Technologies evolve, markets fluctuate and customer expectations transform. However, a leader who does not know how to handle these changes puts the entire organization at risk. Managing change effectively is crucial to the survival and growth of any business.

Change management involves preparing, equipping and supporting employees so that they can successfully adapt to new situations and processes. A leader who is negligent in this regard ignores the importance of preparing his team for change. Instead of guiding and supporting, this leader expects everyone to adapt automatically, as if change were something easy and natural for everyone. This attitude can lead to confusion, resistance, and a drop in employee morale.

Let's imagine a company that decides to implement a new software system to improve operational efficiency. A stupid leader would announce the change overnight, without providing proper training or explaining why the new system is necessary. Employees would find themselves struggling to understand how the software works, making mistakes, and feeling frustrated. Productivity would decrease, and resentment toward leadership would increase. Instead, a competent leader would plan for a gradual implementation, offering ongoing training and support, and clearly communicating the benefits of the new system.

Another facet of change management negligence is a lack of effective communication. A stupid leader does not bother to explain to employees why the change is necessary or how it will be carried out. This lack of information creates a vacuum where uncertainty and rumors can flourish. Employees, without understanding the purpose of the change, may actively resist or, worse yet, feel demotivated and disengaged. Clear, open and consistent communication is essential to reduce anxiety and encourage cooperation during transition periods.

Resistance to change is a natural reaction, and a leader must be prepared to manage it.

A stupid leader may ignore or minimize employee concerns, labeling them as disengagement or negativity. However, these concerns are often valid and deserve to be heard and addressed. A good leader creates spaces for dialogue, actively listens and seeks collaborative solutions. This openness not only makes it easier to adapt to change, but also strengthens the relationship between leadership and the team.

Additionally, a leader who is lax in change management often underestimates the emotional impact that changes can have on employees. Change can cause stress, anxiety and a feeling of loss. A sensitive leader recognizes these emotions and provides the necessary support to help employees navigate these transitions. This can include offering counseling, establishing open communication channels, and making sure employees know that their feelings are valid and that they are not alone.

The impact of change management negligence is not only felt at the individual level, but can also affect the overall performance of the company. Poor change management can result in decreased productivity, increased staff turnover, and a loss of competitiveness in the market. Companies that cannot adapt quickly to new circumstances risk being left behind and, in the worst case, closing their doors.

For example, consider a retail store that doesn't adapt to the growing trend of online shopping. A stupid leader may ignore this tendency, insisting that traditional methods are still sufficient. Meanwhile, competitors adopting e-commerce platforms are beginning to capture greater market share. The store is struggling to attract customers, and may eventually be forced to close due to declining sales.

To avoid this mistake, leaders must take a proactive and systematic approach to change management. This includes carefully planning the change process, clearly communicating goals and benefits, involving employees in the process, providing necessary support and training, and being willing to adjust the plan as necessary. An effective leader understands that change is a continuous process and that success depends on the organization's ability to adapt and evolve.

In short, negligence in change management is a serious mistake that can have devastating consequences for any organization. A stupid leader who does not adequately prepare, support, and communicate during periods of change is dooming his team to failure. Managing change effectively is essential to maintaining competitiveness and ensuring the long-term success of the company. Attentive leadership committed to change management can transform challenges into opportunities and lead the organization towards a promising future.

Micromanagement and Lack of Delegation

One of the most frustrating and demoralizing mistakes a stupid leader can make is micromanagement, or over-managing details, and lack of delegation. These errors not only affect the efficiency of the organization, but also destroy team morale, creating a tense and unproductive work environment.

Micromanagement occurs when a leader insists on supervising and controlling every small detail of his or her employees' work. This type of leader does not trust their team to make decisions or perform tasks on their own. Imagine a conductor who tries to play all the instruments at the same time instead of allowing the musicians to do their job. The result is chaos, and no one can perform properly under so much pressure and control.

A leader who practices micromanagement constantly reviews his employees' work, offers unnecessary criticism, and demands approvals for every small step. This not only slows down progress, but also stifles creativity and initiative. Employees feel as if they are constantly under surveillance and fear making mistakes, which reduces their confidence and autonomy. Instead of focusing on important and strategic tasks, the leader becomes consumed with trivial details, neglecting the true role of guide and mentor to him.

Lack of delegation is another related problem. Delegating is the act of assigning responsibilities and tasks to other team members, trusting in their abilities and judgment to carry them out. A stupid leader, however, has difficulty letting go of control and delegating important tasks. This leader may believe that no one else can do the job as well as him or that delegating is a sign of weakness. However, this mentality is counterproductive.

When a leader does not delegate, he becomes overworked and inefficient. Instead of focusing on strategy and long-term planning, he finds himself caught up in daily tasks that could easily be handled by others. This not only limits growth and innovation, but also puts the health and well-being of the leader at risk. Additionally, employees feel that they are not trusted and do not have the opportunity to develop professionally, leading to high staff turnover and a lack of commitment.

A classic example of micromanagement and lack of delegation could be a project manager who insists on reviewing and approving every email sent by his team. Instead of allowing team members to handle communication themselves, the manager gets involved in every detail, which delays response and creates frustration. The team begins to feel paralyzed, always waiting for manager approval before moving forward, resulting in delayed projects and missed opportunities.

The negative impact of micromanagement and lack of delegation is not just limited to productivity and morale. It can also affect creativity and innovation. When employees do not have the freedom to experiment and make decisions, they become less likely to propose new ideas or solutions. The company, therefore, loses the advantage of having a diverse and talented team that can contribute different perspectives and approaches.

To avoid these mistakes, a leader must learn to trust his team and delegate tasks effectively. This involves identifying the strengths and skills of each team member and assigning them responsibilities that align with those skills. It is also important to set clear expectations and provide the necessary support and resources so employees can fulfill their responsibilities. Effective delegation not only frees up time for the leader, but also empowers employees, fostering a sense of ownership and commitment to their work.

A good leader must also learn to let go of control and allow employees to make decisions and make mistakes. Mistakes are an inevitable part of the learning and growth process. Instead of punishing them, a leader should use them as opportunities to teach and improve. This creates an environment of trust and support, where employees feel safe to take risks and seek innovative solutions.

In short, micromanagement and lack of delegation are mistakes that can have devastating consequences for an organization. A stupid leader who insists on controlling every detail and does not trust his team is condemning his company to inefficiency, demotivation and lack of growth. To be an effective leader, it is essential to learn to delegate responsibilities, trust the team's abilities, and allow employees to make decisions and learn from their experiences. Only in this way can a positive and productive work environment be created, where everyone can contribute to the success of the organization.

Disconnection with Market Needs

One of the most damaging mistakes a stupid leader can make is being disconnected from the needs of the market. In an ever-changing business environment, understanding and adapting to market demands is crucial to success. However, many leaders lock themselves in their offices, relying on their intuition and outdated data instead of keeping up with market trends and expectations. This type of disconnect can lead to poor decisions and the eventual downfall of the company.

The disconnection with the market manifests itself in several ways. First, a leader who does not pay attention to the market may launch products or services that no one wants or needs. Imagine a technology company investing millions into developing a new device, only to discover that consumers are no longer interested in that technology. Without proper market research and listening to customers, the company has wasted valuable resources on something that has no demand.

A real example of this is the case of Blockbuster. In its heyday, Blockbuster was the king of movie rentals. However, its leaders did not see the shift toward online movie streaming. Netflix, on the other hand, understood the changing needs of the market and adapted its business model. While Netflix grew and became a powerhouse in online entertainment, Blockbuster clung to its traditional brick-and-mortar model and ended up disappearing. The lack of vision and adaptation to the needs of the market condemned Blockbuster to failure.

Another way a leader can be out of touch with the market is by not understanding changing consumer preferences. Customer expectations and tastes change over time, and a leader must be attentive to these transformations. For example, in the food industry, today's consumers are looking for healthier and more sustainable options. A company that does not adapt to this trend and continues to offer unhealthy products can quickly lose its customer base to competitors that do respond to these new demands.

Disconnection with the market can also result from a lack of innovation. A stupid leader may be so stuck in existing practices and products that he doesn't realize the need to innovate. Innovation is essential to stay relevant and competitive. However, innovation is not just about creating new products, but also about improving and adapting existing products and services to better meet market needs. A company that does not innovate is destined to stagnate and, eventually, be surpassed by more agile and attentive competitors.

Furthermore, a leader who is disconnected from the market often does not listen to his customers. Customer feedback is an invaluable source of information about what works and what doesn't. Ignoring this feedback is a serious mistake. A leader who does not listen to his customers cannot improve his products or services or solve problems before they become crises. Failure to address customer complaints and suggestions can result in decreased loyalty and a poor reputation.

Disconnection with the market can also lead to poor strategic decision making. Without a clear understanding of the market, a leader can make the wrong investments, choose unsuitable partners, or enter markets that are not profitable. These decisions can have devastating consequences for the company. A classic example is Coca-Cola when it launched "New Coke" in the 1980s. Thinking that consumers wanted a change, the company reformulated its classic recipe. However, consumers rejected the new flavor, and Coca-Cola had to reverse its decision. This disconnection from market preferences cost the company millions of dollars and damaged its image.

To avoid this mistake, leaders must stay connected to the market in several ways. First, they must invest in ongoing market research. This includes surveys, focus groups and data analysis to better understand customers and their changing needs. The information obtained must be used to make informed and strategic decisions.

Second, leaders must foster a culture of active listening within the company. This means valuing and acting on feedback from customers and employees. Employees, who are in direct contact with customers, can provide valuable information on market trends and customer concerns. By valuing these perspectives, a leader can make decisions more aligned with market needs.

Third, leaders must be willing to innovate and adapt. This not only involves developing new products, but also improving and adjusting existing products to better meet market demands. Innovation should be seen as a continuous process and not as a one-time event.

In conclusion, disconnection from market needs is a serious mistake that can lead to obsolescence and failure of any company. A stupid leader who does not pay attention to market trends and demands, who does not listen to his customers and who does not innovate, is condemning his organization to be left behind. To be an effective leader, it is crucial to stay connected to the market, invest in research, actively listen, and be willing to adapt and evolve. Only in this way can long-term success and relevance be ensured in a constantly changing business environment.

Poor Communication

One of the most common and devastating mistakes a stupid leader can make is having poor communication. Communication is the heart of any organization; It's what keeps everyone on the same page, ensures tasks are completed correctly, and allows for quick problem resolution. Without clear and effective communication, an organization can crumble from confusion, misinformation, and lack of direction.

One of the most obvious forms of poor communication is a lack of clarity. A stupid leader often gives vague or contradictory instructions, leaving employees not knowing exactly what is expected of them. For example, he imagines a manager who says, "I want this project done quickly, but make sure you don't make any mistakes." These instructions are confusing because "quickly" and "without errors" can be conflicting goals. Employees, without clear guidance, can feel paralyzed, unsure whether they should prioritize speed or accuracy.

Lack of clarity also manifests itself in the inability to define objectives and expectations. When employees don't know what the organization's goals are or what is expected of them, it is difficult for them to align their efforts with the company's objectives. This can lead to demotivation and low productivity. A good leader must be able to clearly articulate goals and expectations, ensuring that everyone understands and is aligned with the organization's vision.

Another facet of poor communication is lack of feedback. A stupid leader may not give regular or constructive feedback to his employees. Feedback is crucial to the development and growth of employees, as it allows them to know what they are doing well and what areas they need to improve. Without feedback, employees can feel disoriented and unmotivated. For example, if an employee turns in work thinking he has done a good job but receives no feedback, he may continue repeating the same mistakes without knowing it.

Lack of listening is also a big problem. A leader who does not listen to his or her employees creates an environment where employees' ideas and concerns are not valued. This not only demoralizes employees, but also deprives the organization of valuable ideas and solutions. Employees who feel ignored are less likely to contribute new ideas or point out problems that could be avoided. An effective leader must foster a culture of active listening, where employees' opinions and suggestions are valued and considered.

Poor communication can also lead to a lack of transparency. A stupid leader may withhold important information, either due to lack of trust in employees or fear of backlash. However, the lack of transparency generates mistrust and rumors. Employees who do not have access to essential information may feel insecure and distrustful. Transparency, on the other hand, builds trust and loyalty. Sharing relevant information and being honest about the organization's challenges and successes creates a more cohesive and motivated work environment.

A classic example of poor communication is when a company goes through a significant restructuring or change and employees are not adequately informed. Without clear communication, employees can be filled with rumors and assumptions, creating an environment of fear and uncertainty. Instead of focusing on their work, employees are worried about their future and distrust management. An effective leader must communicate openly and honestly, explaining the "what," "why," and "how" of changes, and assuring employees of their value and role in the organization.

Additionally, poor communication can lead to a lack of cohesion and collaboration within the team. When team members do not adequately communicate with each other, misunderstandings and conflicts can arise. Lack of communication can also result in duplication of effort, errors and delays. A leader must foster open and fluid communication within the team, ensuring that everyone is informed and can collaborate effectively.

To improve communication, a leader must develop clear and effective communication skills. This includes the ability to give precise instructions, provide constructive feedback, actively listen, and be transparent. Additionally, it is important to create open and accessible communication channels, where employees feel comfortable sharing their ideas and concerns. Technology can also be a valuable tool to improve communication, through online collaboration tools, virtual meetings and instant messaging platforms.

In short, poor communication is a critical mistake that can have serious consequences for any organization. A stupid leader who does not communicate clearly, does not provide feedback, does not listen and is not transparent is condemning his team to confusion, demotivation and inefficiency. To be an effective leader, it is essential to develop strong communication skills and create an environment where open and honest communication is valued and encouraged. Only through effective communication can team cohesion, productivity and the long-term success of the organization be ensured.

Listening Without Understanding

One of the most insidious and frustrating mistakes a stupid leader can make is listening without understanding. Listening superficially, without really grasping the meaning and emotions behind the words, is a failure that can undermine team morale and lead to poor decisions. This type of leader may believe that he is being approachable and attentive, but in reality, he is missing crucial information and leaving his employees feeling ignored and underestimated.

Listening without understanding is like reading a book without paying attention to the plot or characters. You can run your eyes over the words, but you won't get the gist or important details. Likewise, a leader who only listens superficially may hear his or her employees' words but not understand the context, concerns, or suggestions they are sharing. This lack of understanding can lead to misunderstandings and frustrations that negatively affect team dynamics and the success of the organization.

One of the most common manifestations of listening without understanding is the tendency to interrupt or rush through answers without letting the other person finish speaking. A leader who constantly interrupts is showing that he does not value what his interlocutor has to say. Additionally, by not allowing the message to be completed, the leader may miss important details that could influence his or her understanding and the quality of his or her decisions.

Another way to listen without understanding is to give hasty answers or solutions without taking the time to consider all the implications. For example, if an employee expresses concern about an excessive workload, a leader who listens blankly might simply say, "Work faster" or "Get organized better," without digging into the underlying causes of the problem or offering practical support. Not only is this insensitive, but it also demonstrates a lack of empathy and understanding, which can demotivate the employee and exacerbate the problem.

Listening without understanding can also manifest itself in a lack of following through. A leader may listen to a concern or suggestion, but if he or she doesn't take action or provide feedback, the employee may feel ignored and devalued. Lack of action and response can erode trust and respect for the leader, creating a work environment in which employees do not feel motivated to share their ideas or concerns in the future.

To avoid this mistake, a leader must practice active listening. Active listening involves paying full attention to the interlocutor, without distractions, and striving to really understand what is being said. This includes asking clarifying questions, paraphrasing what has been heard to confirm understanding, and showing empathy toward the other's feelings and concerns. A good leader not only listens to the words, but also picks up the tone, body language, and underlying emotions.

For example, if an employee expresses frustration about the lack of resources to complete a project, a leader who practices active listening might respond: "I understand that you are frustrated by the lack of resources. Can you give me more details about the resources that are available?" need and how are they affecting you?" This response not only shows that the leader has listened, but also demonstrates a genuine interest in understanding and solving the problem.

In addition to active listening, it is important for leaders to foster an environment of open communication. This means creating spaces and moments where employees feel comfortable sharing their ideas and concerns. A leader can organize regular team meetings, feedback sessions, and have an open-door policy. By fostering an environment of open communication, leaders can ensure that they are receiving valuable information and that their employees feel heard and valued.

A classic example of listening without understanding is when an employee expresses concern about work-life balance, and the leader simply responds, "We're all busy, you just have to tough it out." This response not only ignores the employee's legitimate concern, but also shows a lack of empathy and understanding. A leader who truly understands would respond with something like, "I understand that maintaining a work-life balance can be difficult. Can we discuss some ways we can help you better manage your workload?"

Lack of understanding while listening can also lead to ill-informed decisions and a lack of alignment with team goals. A leader who does not understand the true needs and concerns of his or her team may make decisions that do not resolve underlying problems or even make them worse. For example, a leader may implement a new policy to improve productivity without understanding that the true cause of low productivity is a lack of training or resources, not a lack of employee effort.

In short, listening without understanding is a critical mistake that can have devastating consequences for any organization. A stupid leader who only listens superficially, without really grasping the meaning and emotions behind the words, is condemning his team to frustration, demotivation and inefficiency. To be an effective leader, it is essential to practice active listening, show empathy, and foster an environment of open and honest communication. Only then can a true understanding of the team's needs and concerns be ensured, leading to more informed decisions, greater commitment and long-term success.

Inability to Inspire and Motivate

One of the most damaging mistakes a stupid leader can make is the inability to inspire and motivate their team. A leader who does not know how to ignite the spark of inspiration and motivation in his employees is doomed to lead a team that is unmotivated, disengaged, and ultimately ineffective. Inspiring and motivating is not only a desirable skill; It's an absolute must for any leader who wants to see their team thrive and achieve great things.

Inspiration and motivation are the engines that drive productivity and creativity. When employees are inspired, they are more willing to overcome challenges, come up with innovative ideas, and work with passion and dedication. On the other hand, an unmotivated team drags itself through daily tasks, does the minimum necessary and lacks the energy to overcome obstacles. The difference between an inspired team and an unmotivated one can be the difference between success and failure for a project or even an entire company.

A leader who cannot inspire his team often lacks vision. The vision is a clear and compelling picture of what the organization wants to achieve and how it plans to get there. An inspiring leader communicates this vision so that employees can see their role in it and feel part of something bigger than themselves. For example, a leader at a technology company can inspire her team by sharing a vision of how his innovations will change people's lives and improve the world. Without a clear vision, employees can feel as if they are working aimlessly, which can lead to demotivation and apathy.

In addition to vision, a leader must demonstrate passion and enthusiasm for the work. Passion is contagious; When a leader shows genuine enthusiasm for what he does, employees tend to follow his lead. A leader who comes to the office every day with energy and a strong desire to achieve goals can lift the spirits of the entire team. On the other hand, an apathetic or indifferent leader can demotivate even the most enthusiastic employees. A good example of this is a sports coach who shows intense passion and commitment during training and matches, inspiring players to give their best.

The inability to motivate can also be related to a lack of recognition and reward. Employees need to feel valued and appreciated for their work. A simple "thank you" or public recognition can do wonders for team morale. A stupid leader who never recognizes his team's achievements or takes credit for the work of others is undermining his employees' motivation. Rewards don't always have to be monetary; These can be professional development opportunities, additional free time, or even small tokens of appreciation, like a thank-you note.

A good leader also understands the importance of setting clear and achievable goals. Employees feel motivated when they know exactly what is expected of them and can see progress toward their goals. A leader who does not set clear goals leaves employees without a sense of direction, which can lead to frustration and demotivation. Furthermore, it is important that these objectives are achievable; Setting unattainable goals can be discouraging and demoralizing. An inspiring leader ensures that goals are challenging but realistic and celebrates milestones achieved along the way.

Another crucial aspect is employee support and development. A leader must be committed to the growth and professional development of his or her team. This may include offering training opportunities, providing constructive feedback, and helping employees develop their skills and advance their careers. When employees feel that their leader is invested in their personal and professional success, they are more motivated to do their best. A leader who ignores their team's development or doesn't offer support can leave employees feeling stagnant and unmotivated.

Communication also plays a vital role in inspiration and motivation. A leader must be an effective communicator, able to convey vision, objectives and enthusiasm clearly and convincingly. Additionally, he must be willing to listen to employees' ideas and concerns, creating an environment where everyone feels heard and valued. A leader who communicates effectively can inspire trust and loyalty, while one who fails to communicate can generate confusion and distrust.

Finally, an inspirational leader leads by example. Employees look to their leaders for guidance and example. A leader who works hard, demonstrates integrity, and maintains a positive attitude can inspire his team to do the same. Conversely, a leader who exhibits negative behavior, lack of ethics, or laziness can demoralize her team and set a bad example. Leading by example means being consistent in words and actions and demonstrating the values and ethics expected of the team.

In short, the inability to inspire and motivate is a critical mistake that can have serious consequences for any organization. A stupid leader who cannot ignite the spark of inspiration and motivation in his team is condemning his organization to mediocrity and failure. To be an effective leader, it is essential to have a clear vision, demonstrate passion and enthusiasm, recognize and reward employees, set clear objectives, support professional development and communicate effectively. Only through these efforts can a leader inspire and motivate his or her team to achieve great things and ensure the long-term success of the organization.

Ego and Arrogance

Ego and arrogance are two of the worst enemies of effective leadership. A leader with an inflated ego and arrogant attitude can wreak havoc on a team, destroying morale, hindering collaboration, and sabotaging organizational success. A leader's inability to control his ego and maintain humility can have devastating consequences for both the team and the company as a whole.

Ego in leadership manifests itself in many ways, all of them harmful. A leader with an excessive ego tends to believe that he is always right and that his ideas and decisions are superior to those of others. This can lead to ignoring or minimizing the contributions and opinions of team members, creating an environment where people feel undervalued and unmotivated. An arrogant leader who refuses to listen to the ideas of others is closing the door to innovation and continuous improvement. For example, he imagines a manager who insists that his way of doing things is the only correct one and dismisses any suggestions from his employees without even considering them. This not only demotivates the team, but also deprives the organization of valuable insights and solutions.

Arrogance can also manifest itself in a lack of recognition and gratitude. A leader with a big ego may believe that all the organization's successes are the result of her own efforts and fail to recognize the team's contribution. This behavior is extremely demotivating. Employees need to feel that their work is valued and that their efforts are recognized. A leader who takes all the credit for the team's achievements is undermining morale and fostering an environment of resentment and distrust. A classic example is the boss who always takes credit for a successful project without mentioning the hard work of his team, leading to employee demotivation and disengagement.

Ego can also lead to defensive behavior and an inability to admit mistakes. A leader who cannot recognize his own mistakes and learn from them is doomed to repeat them. Humility is an essential quality in a good leader, as it allows for personal and professional growth. An arrogant leader who always blames others or finds excuses for his own failures is creating an environment of fear and lack of responsibility. For example, if a project fails, a humble leader will admit part of the responsibility and work to find solutions and learn from the experience. On the other hand, an arrogant leader will seek to blame others or justify his actions without accepting any blame.

Arrogance can also lead to a lack of empathy. A leader with a big ego may be unable to put himself in his employees' shoes and understand their needs and concerns. Empathy is crucial to building strong, positive relationships within the team. A leader who lacks empathy may appear distant and uninterested in the well-being of their employees, which can lead to demotivation and low morale. An example would be a leader who is unaware of their team's stress and workload and continues to increase demands without offering support or recognition.

Another negative aspect of ego and arrogance is the inability to accept feedback. A leader who is unwilling to listen to constructive criticism and improve is limiting his own growth and that of the organization. Feedback is a valuable tool for development and continuous improvement. A leader who rejects feedback because he believes he is always right is closing the door to improvement and progress. For example, if a leader receives feedback about her communication style and refuses to consider the feedback, he is missing an opportunity to improve his skills and strengthen relationships within the team.

To counteract ego and arrogance, a leader must cultivate humility and self-reflection. Humility involves recognizing that you do not have all the answers and that you can learn from others. A humble leader values and respects the contributions of his team and is willing to listen to and consider different perspectives. Self-reflection allows leaders to critically evaluate their own actions and decisions and look for ways to improve. A leader who practices humility and self-reflection is better equipped to build a strong and successful team.

A good leader must also foster a culture of recognition and gratitude. This means recognizing and celebrating team achievements and showing appreciation for employees' hard work and dedication. A simple gesture of gratitude can have a big impact on team morale and engagement. A leader who shows gratitude and recognition is building a positive and motivating environment where employees feel valued and respected.

Additionally, it is important for leaders to be accessible and open to feedback. This means creating open channels of communication where employees feel comfortable sharing their ideas and concerns. A leader who is willing to listen to and consider feedback is demonstrating respect for her team and a commitment to continuous improvement. This not only strengthens relationships within the team, but also allows the organization to adapt and grow.

In short, ego and arrogance are two of the biggest obstacles to effective leadership. A leader who cannot control his ego and maintain humility is condemning his team to demotivation, lack of innovation and failure. To be an effective leader, it is essential to practice humility, self-reflection, recognition, and openness to feedback. Only through these efforts can a leader build a strong, motivated and successful team, capable of achieving great things and ensuring the long-term success of the organization.

Paulette Durand

Lack of Self-Criticism and Continuous Learning

A leader who does not practice self-criticism and continuous learning stagnates, and with him, his entire team. The lack of self-criticism and a commitment to continuous learning are serious failures that can lead to failure for both the leader and the organization. In this chapter, we'll explore how these flaws affect team dynamics and organizational efficiency, and why it's crucial for leaders to strive for constant improvement.

Self-criticism is the ability to honestly evaluate one's own actions and decisions. A leader who lacks self-criticism is like a captain who navigates without a map or a compass; He has no way to correct course when he strays. Self-criticism allows leaders to recognize their mistakes, learn from them, and make necessary adjustments to improve. Without this skill, a leader becomes his own worst enemy, repeating the same mistakes over and over again without learning anything in the process.

A leader without self-criticism tends to blame others for his failures. For example, if a project fails, instead of analyzing what decisions could have contributed to the failure and how things could have been done differently, a leader without self-criticism will look for blame among team members. This attitude is not only unfair, but it also creates an environment of fear and mistrust, where employees are afraid to take risks or make decisions for fear of being punished for the leader's mistakes.

Lack of self-criticism can also lead to a disconnection from reality. A leader who does not take the time to reflect on his or her performance and listen to the opinions of his or her team may lose sight of what is really happening in the organization. This can result in ill-informed decisions and strategies that do not align with current needs and challenges. For example, a leader who doesn't realize that her authoritarian management style is demotivating her team may continue to implement policies that exacerbate the problem, instead of looking for ways to foster a more collaborative and motivating work environment.

Continuous learning is equally crucial to leadership success. In a rapidly changing world, yesterday's skills and knowledge may not be enough to meet the challenges of today and tomorrow. A leader who does not commit to continuous learning risks falling behind, both in terms of technical skills and management strategies. Lack of continuous learning can result in a lack of innovation and an inability to adapt to new circumstances, which can be fatal for the organization.

A leader committed to continuous learning actively seeks opportunities to improve and expand his or her knowledge. This may include reading books and articles, attending conferences and seminars, participating in courses and workshops, and seeking mentorship. An example of a leader who practices continuous learning is someone who, when faced with a technological challenge in her company, decides to take a course on the new technology instead of relying solely on her team to solve it. By doing so, he not only improves his own skills, but also shows his team the importance of continuous training and development.

Continuous learning also means being open to new ideas and perspectives. A leader who surrounds himself with people with different experiences and knowledge and who is willing to listen and learn from them is better prepared to make informed and strategic decisions. For example, a leader in a global company can benefit greatly from learning about different international cultures and markets, allowing them to adapt the company's strategies to various realities and needs.

A lack of self-criticism and continuous learning can also affect a leader's ability to innovate. Innovation requires the ability to question the status quo and look for new and better ways of doing things. A leader who is not self-critical or committed to continuous learning may feel comfortable with the way things have always been done and resist change. This can lead to obsolescence and a loss of competitiveness in a constantly evolving market.

To counteract a lack of self-criticism and encourage continuous learning, leaders must cultivate a growth mindset. This means always being willing to learn and improve, and seeing mistakes and challenges as opportunities for development. A leader with a growth mindset seeks constructive feedback and is willing to make the necessary changes to improve her performance. For example, a leader can regularly ask his team for feedback on his management style and use this information to make adjustments that benefit everyone.

Additionally, leaders must create an organizational culture that values and encourages continuous learning. This may include offering training and development opportunities to employees, promoting collaboration and knowledge sharing, and recognizing and rewarding those who demonstrate a commitment to their own development and that of the organization. An example of this is a company that provides an annual budget for employees to attend courses and conferences, and that celebrates the achievements of those who acquire new skills and knowledge.

In short, a lack of self-criticism and continuous learning are serious failures that can have devastating consequences for leadership and the organization. A leader who does not practice self-criticism is unable to recognize and learn from his mistakes, leading to misinformed decisions and a toxic work environment. Likewise, a leader who does not commit to continuous learning risks being left behind in an ever-changing world. To be an effective leader, it is essential to cultivate self-criticism, foster a growth mindset, and create an organizational culture that values and promotes continuous learning. Only through these efforts can leaders ensure the long-term success and sustainability of their team and the organization.

Dishonesty and Lack of Integrity

Dishonesty and lack of integrity are poisons to any type of leadership. A leader who does not act with honesty and maintain integrity is condemning his team to an environment of distrust, resentment and, ultimately, failure. Integrity is the cornerstone of a good working relationship and without it, everything else falls apart. In this chapter, we will explore how dishonesty and a lack of integrity can destroy leadership and why it is crucial that leaders strive to be honest and maintain high ethical standards.

Dishonesty can manifest itself in many ways in leadership. It can be through outright lies, omissions of the truth, or empty promises that are never fulfilled. A leader who lies to his team is sowing the seeds of distrust. When employees discover that they have been deceived, their trust in the leader is broken and it is very difficult, if not impossible, to rebuild that trust. A clear example is a leader who promises salary increases or promotions without having the real intention of following through on those promises. When employees realize that these promises were empty, they feel betrayed and demotivated.

Lack of integrity also manifests itself in inconsistency between a leader's words and actions. A leader of integrity not only says the right thing, but also acts on his words. Integrity means being consistent and maintaining the same standards in all circumstances, even when it is difficult. A leader who does not practice what he preaches is sending a message of hypocrisy and lack of commitment to the values he claims to defend. For example, a leader who talks about the importance of teamwork, but makes decisions unilaterally without consulting her team, is demonstrating a lack of integrity.

Dishonesty and lack of integrity can also erode organizational culture. The culture of an organization is largely shaped by the behavior of its leaders. If a leader acts dishonestly, this behavior is likely to spread and become the accepted norm within the organization. This can lead to a toxic environment where employees feel pressured to act dishonestly to meet expectations or to advance their careers. An example is a company where leaders falsify reports or manipulate data to show better results than actually exist. This culture of dishonesty can eventually lead to legal consequences and loss of reputation.

Lack of integrity also affects decision making. A leader who does not act with integrity may make decisions based on self-interest rather than what is best for the team or organization. This can lead to short-term decisions that harm the organization in the long term. An example of this is a leader who decides to reduce costs by laying off key employees without considering the negative impact this will have on the morale and operational capacity of the team.

To counter dishonesty and lack of integrity, it is essential that leaders commit to transparency and honesty in all their interactions. Transparency means being open and clear about decisions, policies and expectations. A transparent leader shares relevant information with his team and explains the reasoning behind his decisions. This not only builds trust, but also allows employees to understand and align with the organization's vision and goals. An example of transparency is a leader who communicates clearly and honestly about the challenges facing the organization and works together with the organization's team to find solutions.

Honesty also means admitting mistakes and taking responsibility for one's actions. A leader who can recognize when he has made a mistake and is willing to learn from his mistakes is demonstrating integrity and earning the respect of his team. This not only strengthens trust, but also creates an environment where employees feel safe to make mistakes and learn from them without fear of retaliation. A leader who admits his mistakes and works to correct them is setting a positive example for the entire team.

Additionally, leaders must establish and maintain high ethical standards. This means not only acting with integrity in all situations, but also demanding the same level of integrity from all team members. An ethical leader does not tolerate dishonest behavior and takes steps to address any lack of integrity within the team. This may include implementing clear policies on ethics and conduct, as well as training and support to help employees understand and comply with these standards.

Integrity is also reflected in the way a leader treats others. A leader of integrity respects all team members and treats them fairly and equitably. This includes being honest and direct in feedback, recognizing and celebrating employees' achievements, and supporting their professional development and growth. A leader who demonstrates respect and fairness is building a positive and motivating work environment where employees feel valued and respected.

Finally, it is important for leaders to practice self-reflection and actively seek ways to improve their own integrity and honesty. This may include seeking mentorship and guidance from other respected leaders, participating in leadership development programs, and seeking feedback from employees and colleagues. A leader who is committed to continually improving his or her own integrity and honesty is demonstrating a strong commitment to the values and principles that are essential to effective leadership.

In short, dishonesty and lack of integrity are two of the biggest obstacles to effective leadership. A leader who does not act with honesty and does not maintain an upright conduct is condemning his team to an environment of mistrust and demotivation. To be an effective leader, it is essential to practice transparency, honesty, self-reflection, and maintain high ethical standards. Only through these efforts can a leader build a strong, confident and motivated team, capable of achieving great things and ensuring the long-term success of the organization.

Lack of Empathy and Consideration

Empathy and consideration are essential for any leader who aspires to be effective and respected. The absence of these qualities can cause serious problems in a team and in the organization in general. A leader who does not show empathy or consideration toward his or her employees can create a negative work environment, affect team morale, and decrease productivity. In this chapter, we will explore how a lack of empathy and consideration can impair leadership and why it is essential for leaders to develop these qualities.

Empathy is the ability to understand and share the feelings of others. It's putting yourself in someone else's shoes and seeing things from their perspective. An empathetic leader can better connect with his or her team, understand their needs and concerns, and respond appropriately. However, a leader who lacks empathy may appear distant and uninterested in the well-being of their employees, which can lead to demotivation and dissatisfaction.

For example, imagine a leader who never takes the time to ask his employees how they are doing or if they need any support. This leader only focuses on the results and the numbers, without worrying about the people behind those numbers. Employees may feel like mere cogs in a machine, rather than human beings valued for their work and effort. This can lead to high staff turnover, as employees seek a work environment where they feel appreciated and understood.

Consideration, on the other hand, is the action of taking the feelings and needs of others into account in daily decisions and actions. A thoughtful leader thinks about how his decisions will affect his team and makes a conscious effort to minimize any negative impact. Lack of consideration can manifest itself in many ways, such as imposing unreasonable deadlines, failing to recognize hard work, or indifference to employees' personal problems.

For example, a leader who constantly demands overtime without considering his or her employees' work-life balance is demonstrating a lack of consideration. This can lead to burnout and stress, which in turn can negatively impact productivity and quality of work. A thoughtful leader, on the other hand, looks for ways to balance the demands of the job with the personal needs of employees, promoting a healthy and sustainable work environment.

The absence of empathy and consideration can also affect communication within the team. A leader who does not listen to his employees or who dismisses her concerns is closing the door to open and honest communication. This can lead to misunderstandings, resentments and a lack of trust. For example, if an employee feels ignored or undervalued, he may stop sharing important ideas or concerns, which can result in undetected problems and missed opportunities.

Empathy and consideration are especially important in times of change or crisis. During these times, employees may feel insecure and stressed, and an empathetic leader can help alleviate those concerns by demonstrating understanding and support. A leader who lacks empathy can aggravate the situation by not recognizing or responding appropriately to the emotions and needs of his team.

To develop empathy and consideration, leaders must practice active listening. This means paying full attention to what employees are saying, without interruptions or distractions, and showing genuine interest in their concerns and opinions. Active listening also involves asking clarifying questions and demonstrating that you have understood what has been said. A leader who practices active listening is building an environment of trust and mutual respect.

Another way to show empathy and consideration is through recognition and appreciation. Leaders should take the time to recognize and celebrate their employees' achievements and efforts. This can be as simple as a verbal thank you or public recognition in a team meeting. Recognition shows employees that their work is valued and appreciated, which can increase morale and engagement.

Empathy and consideration are also reflected in how leaders manage work-life balance. Leaders must be aware of the demands they place on their employees and make efforts to promote a healthy balance. This may include implementing flexible working policies, promoting regular breaks and respecting employees' free time. A leader who values and respects work-life balance is demonstrating consideration for the well-being of her team.

Additionally, leaders must be willing to support their employees during difficult times. This may include offering emotional support, providing stress management resources, or being flexible with schedules in difficult personal situations. A leader who shows support in difficult times is building loyalty and commitment among his employees.

In short, the absence of empathy and consideration can have serious consequences for leadership and the organization. A leader who does not show empathy can appear distant and disinterested, which can lead to employee demotivation and dissatisfaction. Lack of consideration can result in decisions and actions that negatively affect employees and the work environment. To be an effective leader, it is essential to develop empathy and consideration through active listening, recognition, and promoting a healthy work-life balance. Only through these efforts can leaders build a strong, motivated and successful team, capable of achieving great things and ensuring the long-term success of the organization.

Toxic Work Climate

A toxic work environment is one of the biggest obstacles to the success of any organization. A leader who does not care about the work environment can create an environment where stress, demotivation, and conflict become the norm. A toxic work environment not only affects employee morale and productivity, but can also lead to high employee turnover and health problems. In this chapter, we will explore how poor leadership can contribute to a toxic work environment and why it is crucial that leaders strive to create a positive and healthy work environment.

A toxic work environment is characterized by the presence of negative behaviors such as harassment, intimidation, favoritism, and lack of respect. These behaviors can arise when a leader does not establish and maintain high standards of behavior in the workplace. For example, if a leader allows certain employees to harass or bully others without consequences, she is sending the message that this type of behavior is acceptable. This not only affects the direct victims, but also creates an environment of fear and insecurity for all employees.

Additionally, a leader who does not adequately manage conflict can contribute to a toxic work environment. Conflicts are inevitable in any work environment, but it is how they are handled that determines whether the work environment remains healthy or becomes toxic. A leader who ignores conflict or takes sides unfairly can exacerbate problems and create divisions within the team. For example, if a leader always takes sides with the same employees, regardless of the merits of the situation, other employees may feel devalued and demotivated.

A lack of open and honest communication can also contribute to a toxic work environment. When employees feel that they cannot express their opinions or concerns without fear of retaliation, an environment of silence and resentment is created. A leader who does not encourage open communication is depriving his team of the opportunity to constructively solve problems and continually improve. For example, if employees feel that their suggestions are constantly ignored or dismissed, they may stop trying to contribute, which negatively affects innovation and team performance.

Favoritism is another factor that can create a toxic work environment. When a leader shows preferential treatment to certain employees, whether through opportunities, recognition, or benefits, it creates an environment of inequity and resentment. Employees who are not treated equally may feel undervalued and demotivated, which can lead to a decrease in productivity and an increase in employee turnover. For example, if a leader always assigns the most interesting and challenging projects to the same employees, others may feel left out and belittled.

Lack of support and recognition can also contribute to a toxic work environment. Employees need to feel that their work is valued and appreciated. A leader who does not recognize the achievements and efforts of her team is sending the message that hard work does not matter. This can lead to demotivation and a decrease in the quality of work. For example, if a leader never takes the time to thank his employees for their efforts or to celebrate their achievements, employees may feel invisible and unappreciated.

Excessive stress is another key component of a toxic work environment. A leader who imposes unreasonable deadlines, excessive workload, and unrealistic expectations is creating an environment of chronic stress. This not only affects the mental and physical health of employees, but can also lead to a decrease in productivity and quality of work. For example, if a leader always expects employees to work overtime and weekends without regard for their work-life balance, employees may burn out and seek employment elsewhere.

To counteract a toxic work environment, leaders must strive to create a positive and healthy work environment. This begins with establishing and promoting high standards of conduct. Leaders must make it clear that harassment, bullying and disrespect will not be tolerated, and must take firm and fair action to address any inappropriate behavior. This may include implementing clear policies, training in communication and conflict resolution skills, and creating a confidential reporting system.

Open and honest communication is essential to a positive work environment. Leaders must foster a culture where employees feel safe to express their opinions and concerns. This may include holding regular feedback meetings, creating open communication channels, and demonstrating a receptive and respectful attitude toward suggestions and criticism. An example of this is a leader who organizes regular meetings where employees can share their ideas and concerns without fear of retaliation, and who takes seriously and acts on feedback received.

Recognition and support are equally important. Leaders should take the time to recognize and celebrate their employees' achievements, and to offer support and resources when needed. This may include implementing recognition programs, providing professional development opportunities, and creating an environment where employees feel valued and appreciated. An example is a leader who regularly celebrates team successes with special events, meeting mentions, and professional growth opportunities.

Proper stress management is also crucial. Leaders should be aware of workloads and expectations, and should strive to promote a healthy work-life balance. This may include implementing flexible working policies, promoting regular breaks and supporting employees with stress management. An example is a leader who promotes the use of time off and provides resources such as wellness programs and counseling to help employees manage stress.

In short, a toxic work environment can have devastating consequences for any organization. A leader who does not care about the work environment is contributing to an environment where stress, demotivation and conflict are the norm. To be an effective leader, it is essential to create a positive and healthy work environment by establishing high standards of behavior, promoting open communication, recognizing and supporting employees, and appropriately managing stress. Only through these efforts can leaders ensure the success and well-being of their team and the organization as a whole.

High Staff Turnover

High staff turnover is one of the most obvious signs that something is not working well in an organization. When employees leave frequently, it is a sign that they are dissatisfied with the work environment, company culture, or management. This issue can be extremely costly for businesses, not only in terms of money, but also in terms of time and resources. In this chapter, we'll explore how poor leadership can contribute to high employee turnover and why it's crucial for leaders to address this issue effectively.

Employee turnover refers to the rate at which employees leave a company and are replaced by new employees. A high turnover rate means that many employees are leaving the company in a short period of time. This can be devastating for an organization because every time an employee leaves, the investment the company made in their training and development is lost. Additionally, the process of recruiting, hiring, and training new employees is costly and time-consuming.

One of the main reasons employees leave a company is because they are unhappy with its leadership. A leader who doesn't listen to their employees, support them, or provide them with opportunities for growth can leave employees feeling undervalued and demotivated. For example, a leader who never recognizes his employees' achievements or does not provide them with constructive feedback is creating an environment where employees do not feel appreciated or valued. This can lead employees to seek other opportunities where they feel more appreciated and have better growth prospects.

Another factor that contributes to high employee turnover is a lack of work-life balance. Employees who feel constantly stressed and overworked are more likely to leave the company in search of a more balanced work environment. A leader who does not promote work-life balance is sending the message that employee well-being is not a priority. For example, if a leader expects employees to work long hours and weekends without regard for their personal time, employees may feel exhausted and burned out, making them more likely to seek employment elsewhere.

Lack of professional development opportunities can also lead to high staff turnover. Employees want to feel like they are growing and advancing in their careers. A leader who doesn't offer professional development opportunities, such as training, mentoring, or promotions, is creating an environment where employees feel stuck. For example, if a leader never offers employees the opportunity to learn new skills or take on new responsibilities, employees may feel like they have no future at the company and will look for growth opportunities elsewhere.

The toxic work environment, which we talked about in the previous chapter, is another factor that can contribute to high staff turnover. A work environment where there is harassment, intimidation, favoritism, and disrespect can make employees feel uncomfortable and demotivated. A leader who does not address these issues is allowing the work environment to deteriorate, which may lead to employees deciding to leave. For example, if a leader allows certain employees to behave inappropriately without consequences, other employees may feel that the work environment is unfair and unsafe, making them more likely to leave.

Additionally, the lack of competitive compensation and benefits can be a major reason for high employee turnover. Employees want to feel fairly compensated for their work. A leader who does not ensure that employees receive competitive compensation and benefits is at risk of losing valuable talent. For example, if a leader does not regularly review and adjust salaries and benefits to ensure they are competitive with the market, employees may feel underpaid and seek employment at other companies that offer better compensation.

To address the problem of high employee turnover, leaders must focus on creating a positive work environment and meeting the needs and expectations of their employees. This starts with active listening and open communication. Leaders must take the time to listen to their employees, understand their concerns, and respond appropriately. For example, a leader who holds regular feedback meetings and demonstrates that he values and acts on his employees' feedback is building a work environment where employees feel heard and valued.

Recognition and appreciation are also crucial to retaining employees. Leaders should take the time to recognize and celebrate their employees' achievements. This can include public recognition at team meetings, employee of the month awards, or simply a verbal thank you. For example, a leader who regularly takes the time to thank his employees for their hard work and dedication is showing that he values her contribution, which can increase employee morale and engagement.

Work-life balance is another important aspect. Leaders must promote a work environment where employees can balance their work and personal responsibilities. This may include flexible work policies, such as teleworking or flexible hours, and the promotion of regular breaks and time off. For example, a leader who encourages his employees to take vacations and disconnect from work outside of work hours is showing that he values their well-being, which can reduce stress and burnout.

Professional development opportunities are also essential for retaining employees. Leaders must provide their employees with the tools and resources necessary to grow and advance in their careers. This may include training programs, mentoring, and promotion opportunities. For example, a leader who regularly offers training and development sessions, and who promotes talented employees to positions of greater responsibility, is showing that she values the growth and development of her team.

Finally, competitive compensation and benefits are crucial to retaining employees. Leaders must ensure that the salaries and benefits they offer are competitive with the market. This may include regular salary reviews, bonuses, and additional benefits such as health insurance and retirement plans. For example, a leader who regularly reviews and adjusts salaries to ensure they are aligned with market trends is demonstrating that he appropriately values and rewards his employees' work.

In summary, high employee turnover is a significant problem that can have serious consequences for any organization. Poor leadership can contribute to this problem by not meeting employee needs and expectations. To address high employee turnover, leaders should focus on creating a positive work environment, listening to and recognizing their employees, promoting work-life balance, providing professional development opportunities, and ensuring a competitive compensation and benefits. By doing so, leaders can retain valuable talent, increase employee morale and engagement, and ensure the long-term success of the organization.

Loss of Talent

Talent loss is one of the most critical challenges an organization can face. When talented employees leave, the company loses not only their skills and knowledge, but also the investment made in their training and development. Additionally, the departure of key personnel can affect team morale and productivity. In this chapter, we'll explore how poor leadership can contribute to talent loss and why it's crucial for leaders to work to retain their best employees.

Talented employees are the heart of any successful organization. They are those who contribute innovative ideas, lead important projects and help the company achieve its objectives. However, when these employees do not feel valued or supported, they are likely to seek opportunities elsewhere where they feel more appreciated. A leader who does not recognize and reward talent is at risk of losing his best employees. For example, if a leader never praises employees for good work or does not offer them opportunities for advancement, employees may feel that their efforts are not appreciated and will seek employment elsewhere.

One of the main reasons talented employees leave a company is a lack of career development opportunities. Talented employees want to grow and advance in their careers. If they feel like they are stuck in their current position with no chance of advancement, they are likely to look for a company that offers them better opportunities. A leader who does not focus on the professional development of his employees is sending the message that growth is not a priority. For example, if a leader does not offer training or mentoring programs, employees may feel frustrated by the lack of opportunities to learn and improve their skills.

Another factor that contributes to the loss of talent is the lack of recognition and rewards. Talented employees want to know that their hard work and achievements are appreciated. A leader who does not take the time to recognize and celebrate their employees' successes is creating an environment where employees can feel invisible and undervalued. For example, if a leader never thanks or celebrates his team's achievements, employees may feel that their work is unimportant and will look for a company that values their contribution more.

Work-life balance is also crucial to retaining talented employees. Employees want to work in an environment where their personal time is respected and a healthy balance is promoted. A leader who imposes unreasonable workloads and does not allow flexibility is creating an environment where employees can feel stressed and burned out. For example, if a leader expects employees to work long hours without time to rest and recharge, employees may feel that their well-being is not a priority and will seek employment elsewhere that offers a better work-life balance. .

Company culture also plays an important role in retaining talent. Talented employees want to work in an environment where they feel part of a team and where collaboration and mutual respect are promoted. A leader who does not focus on building a positive and supportive culture is at risk of losing their best employees. For example, if a leader allows a toxic work environment where harassment and disrespect are prevalent, employees may feel uncomfortable and unsafe and will seek out a company with a more positive culture.

Additionally, the lack of competitive compensation and benefits can lead to loss of talent. Talented employees know their value and want to be compensated fairly for their skills and efforts. A leader who does not ensure that salaries and benefits are competitive with the market is at risk of losing his best employees. For example, if a leader does not regularly review and adjust salaries to keep up with market trends, employees may feel underpaid and will seek employment with a company that offers better compensation.

To retain talented employees, leaders must focus on creating a positive work environment and meeting the needs and expectations of their employees. This begins with recognition and appreciation. Leaders should take the time to recognize and celebrate their employees' achievements. This can include public recognition at team meetings, employee of the month awards, or simply a verbal thank you. For example, a leader who regularly takes the time to thank his employees for their hard work and dedication is showing that he values her contribution, which can increase employee morale and engagement.

Professional development is also crucial to retaining talented employees. Leaders must provide their employees with the tools and resources necessary to grow and advance in their careers. This may include training programs, mentoring, and promotion opportunities. For example, a leader who regularly offers training and development sessions, and who promotes talented employees to positions of greater responsibility, is showing that she values the growth and development of her team.

Work-life balance is another important aspect. Leaders must promote a work environment where employees can balance their work and personal responsibilities. This may include flexible work policies, such as teleworking or flexible hours, and the promotion of regular breaks and time off. For example, a leader who encourages his employees to take vacations and disconnect from work outside of work hours is showing that he values their well-being, which can reduce stress and burnout.

Company culture is also essential for retaining talented employees. Leaders should focus on building a positive, supportive culture where employees feel part of a team and collaboration and mutual respect are promoted. This may include creating opportunities for teamwork, promoting shared values, and fostering an inclusive and respectful work environment. For example, a leader who organizes team activities and promotes a culture of respect and support is creating an environment where employees feel valued and connected.

Finally, competitive compensation and benefits are crucial to retaining talented employees. Leaders must ensure that the salaries and benefits they offer are competitive with the market. This may include regular salary reviews, bonuses, and additional benefits such as health insurance and retirement plans. For example, a leader who regularly reviews and adjusts salaries to ensure they are aligned with market trends is demonstrating that he appropriately values and rewards his employees' work.

In short, talent loss is a significant problem that can have serious consequences for any organization. Poor leadership can contribute to this problem by not meeting employee needs and expectations. To retain talented employees, leaders must focus on creating a positive work environment, recognizing and appreciating their employees, providing professional development opportunities, promoting work-life balance, building a culture of positive business and ensuring competitive compensation and benefits. By doing so, leaders can retain valuable talent, increase employee morale and engagement, and ensure the long-term success of the organization.

Reputation and Trust Crisis

Reputation and trust are two fundamental pillars for the success of any organization. When these pillars are compromised, the consequences can be devastating. A reputation crisis can erode the trust of customers, employees and investors, seriously affecting the performance and survival of the company. In this chapter, we will explore how poor leadership can trigger a crisis of reputation and trust, and why it is crucial for leaders to keep these elements intact.

A reputation crisis occurs when a company's public image is damaged, whether by inappropriate actions, scandals, or poor decisions. Trust, on the other hand, refers to the faith that stakeholders have in the company and its leaders. Both aspects are intrinsically related; Once reputation is damaged, trust is also affected. For example, if a company is involved in a financial fraud scandal, customers may lose trust in the company and decide to take their business elsewhere.

A leader plays a crucial role in managing a company's reputation and trust. His decisions, actions and behaviors have a direct impact on how the company is perceived by the public. A leader who acts ethically, transparently and responsibly helps build and maintain a good reputation. Conversely, a leader who makes questionable decisions, hides information, or acts irresponsibly can trigger a reputation crisis. For example, if a leader decides to cut costs at the expense of product quality, customers may feel cheated and disappointed, which can damage the company's reputation.

Lack of transparency is one of the biggest catalysts for a reputation crisis. Stakeholders expect companies to be open and honest about their operations, policies and issues. A leader who hides information or distorts the truth is putting the company's reputation at risk. For example, if a company faces a quality problem with one of its products and the leader decides to hide the problem rather than address it openly, customers may feel betrayed when they learn the truth, which can lead to a loss of trust. and reputation.

Crisis management is another crucial aspect of maintaining reputation and trust.

At some point, every business faces challenges and problems. What separates successful companies from those that fail is how they handle those crises. An effective leader must be able to act quickly, communicate clearly, and make responsible decisions to mitigate damage. For example, if a company faces a data security breach, a leader who responds quickly, informs those affected, and takes corrective action can protect the company's reputation and maintain customer trust.

Consistency between the leader's words and actions is also essential to maintaining reputation and trust. Stakeholders judge companies not only by what they say, but also by what they do. A leader who preaches values of integrity and responsibility, but acts in a contrary way, is sending contradictory messages that can erode trust. For example, if a leader promotes the importance of sustainability but the company continues harmful environmental practices, customers and employees may perceive a lack of authenticity and trust in the company.

Corporate social responsibility (CSR) is another factor that influences reputation and trust. Today's consumers and employees expect companies to not only focus on profits, but also to commit to social and environmental causes. A leader who integrates CSR into the company's strategy is helping to build a positive reputation and gain the trust of stakeholders. For example, a company that engages in community initiatives, reduces its carbon footprint, and treats its employees fairly is demonstrating a commitment to the well-being of society and the environment, which can improve its reputation and earn loyalty. of the clients.

Effective communication is essential to manage reputation and trust. Leaders must be clear, honest and consistent in their communications with stakeholders. This includes being proactive in communicating good and bad news, and ensuring messages are understandable and accessible. For example, if a company is experiencing financial difficulties, a leader who openly communicates the challenges and plans to address them can maintain the trust of employees and investors, even in difficult times.

Organizational culture also plays an important role in reputation and trust. A strong culture, based on ethical values and responsibility, reinforces the company's positive reputation and fosters trust among employees and other stakeholders. A leader who promotes and lives these values is building a strong foundation for the company's reputation and trust. For example, if a leader fosters a culture of inclusion and respect, employees will feel valued and engaged, which in turn can improve the external perception of the company.

Mistakes are inevitable, but how a leader handles them can make the difference between a reputation crisis and an opportunity for empowerment. Leaders must be able to admit mistakes, learn from them, and take steps to prevent them from happening again. This not only shows accountability and transparency, but can also reinforce trust. For example, if a leader admits a mistake in the company's strategy and presents a clear plan to correct it, stakeholders may see this as a sign of integrity and commitment, which can strengthen trust in leadership.

Business ethics are the basis of a good reputation and trust. Leaders must make decisions based on ethical principles and consider the impact of their actions on all stakeholders. A leader who adheres to high ethical standards is building a solid foundation for reputation and trust. For example, if a leader decides to reject a lucrative contract because it involves unethical practices, he is demonstrating that the company values integrity more than short-term profits, which can improve reputation and gain the trust of stakeholders.

In short, the crisis of reputation and trust is a serious problem that can have lasting consequences for any organization. Poor leadership can trigger and aggravate this crisis by failing to act ethically, transparently and responsibly. To avoid a reputation crisis and maintain trust, leaders must focus on transparency, effective crisis management, consistency between words and actions, corporate social responsibility, effective communication, organizational culture, proper error management and adherence to high ethical standards. By doing so, leaders can build and maintain a positive reputation and stakeholder trust, ensuring the long-term success and sustainability of the organization.

Lessons Learned and Paths to Improvement

Experience is an invaluable teacher, and many valuable lessons can be learned from leadership mistakes. In this chapter, we will explore lessons learned from common leaders' mistakes and outline paths to improvement. The key is to recognize areas of opportunity, adopt a growth mindset, and apply strategic changes to become a more effective and respected leader.

First, it is essential to recognize that no one is perfect. All leaders make mistakes at some point in their career. The difference between a good leader and a mediocre leader lies in how they handle those mistakes. An effective leader is able to admit his or her failures, learn from them, and take steps to prevent them from happening again. For example, if a leader realizes that he has been making impulsive decisions without sufficient data, he can commit to taking a more analytical and evidence-based approach to future decisions.

One of the most important lessons is the importance of effective communication. Many problems in leadership arise from poor communication. Leaders must be clear, honest and open in their communications with the team. This includes not only conveying information clearly, but also actively listening to employees and considering their opinions and concerns. For example, a leader who improves his or her listening skills can identify problems before they become crises and take preventive action.

Another crucial learning is the need for strategic planning. Lack of vision and planning can lead to disorganization and failure. Leaders must take the time to develop a clear vision for the future of the organization and chart a strategic path to achieve that vision. This includes setting short- and long-term goals, identifying necessary resources, and designing concrete action plans. For example, a leader who spends time on strategic planning can guide her team toward clear, achievable goals, increasing the organization's overall efficiency and success.

Change management is another critical area for improvement. Change is inevitable in any organization, and leaders must be able to manage it effectively. This involves preparing employees for the change, clearly communicating the reasons behind the change, and supporting employees during the transition process. For example, a leader who implements training programs to help employees adapt to new technologies can reduce resistance to change and increase the adoption and effectiveness of new tools.

Delegating responsibilities is an essential skill that many leaders need to improve. Micromanagement can stifle employee creativity and autonomy, leading to dissatisfaction and low productivity. Leaders must learn to trust their team and delegate tasks effectively. This not only eases the burden on the leader, but also empowers employees and encourages their professional development. For example, a leader who delegates important projects to her employees shows confidence in her abilities and allows the team to grow and develop.

Empathy and consideration for employees are essential for effective leadership. Leaders should strive to understand their employees' needs and concerns and show empathy in their daily interactions. This creates a positive work environment and increases employee loyalty and engagement. For example, a leader who shows empathy and support to an employee who is going through a difficult personal situation can strengthen the relationship and foster a greater sense of belonging among the team.

The importance of integrity and honesty cannot be underestimated. Leaders who act with integrity and transparency earn the trust and respect of their employees, customers and investors. Dishonesty and a lack of integrity, on the other hand, can quickly erode trust and damage a company's reputation. For example, a leader who always acts honestly, even when faced with difficult decisions, is setting an ethical standard that others will follow.

Continuous learning and self-criticism are essential components of leadership growth. Leaders must be willing to learn new skills, adapt to changes, and accept constructive criticism. This involves participating in professional development programs, seeking regular feedback, and being open to new ideas and approaches. For example, a leader who attends leadership workshops and actively seeks feedback from her team is demonstrating a commitment to growth and continuous improvement.

Recognizing and rewarding talent is another important area. Leaders should strive to recognize and celebrate their employees' achievements. This may include public praise, awards, and professional development opportunities. Recognition not only motivates employees, but also shows that the leader values their contribution. For example, a leader who implements a monthly recognition program to highlight employees' outstanding work is fostering a positive and motivating work environment.

Finally, building and maintaining a positive organizational culture is critical to long-term success. Leaders must promote values such as collaboration, respect and inclusion, and ensure that these values are reflected in all areas of the organization. A strong, positive organizational culture not only attracts talent, but also retains employees and improves overall performance. For example, a leader who encourages collaboration and mutual respect in the workplace is creating an environment where employees feel valued and motivated to contribute to the company's goals.

In conclusion, leadership mistakes can be valuable learning opportunities. By acknowledging mistakes, learning from them, and taking steps to improve, leaders can become more effective versions of themselves. Effective communication, strategic planning, change management, delegation, empathy, integrity, continuous learning, talent recognition and building a positive organizational culture are all key aspects that leaders must address to improve and succeed. By doing so, they not only benefit themselves, but also their teams and the organization as a whole, creating a more productive, positive and successful work environment.